One
Dish
Meals

Library of Congress Cataloging-in-Publication Data

De Villiers, Stoffelina Johanna Adriana.
   One dish meals.

   (First cookbook library / S.J.A. de Villiers and
E. van der Berg)
   Includes index.
   Summary: Introduces the young chef to one dish
meals.
      1. Casserole cookery—Juvenile literature.
[1. Casserole cookery. 2. Cookery] I. Van der Berg,
Eunice. II. Johnson, Marita, ill. III. Title.
IV. Series: De Villiers, Stoffelina Johanna Adriana.
First cookbook library.

TX693.D35 1985   641.8'2   85-12699
ISBN 0-918831-76-8
ISBN 0-918831-31-8 (lib. bdg.)

ISBN 0-918831-31-8 lib. bdg.
ISBN 0-918831-76-8 trade bdg.

U.S. Edition Copyright © 1985 by Gareth Stevens, Inc.

First published in *It's Fun to Cook* by Daan Retief Publishers
Copyright © 1983

Series Editors: MaryLee Knowlton
Cover Illustrations: Renée Graef
Typeset by Superior Printing • Milwaukee, Wisconsin 53223, USA

One Dish Meals

S.J.A. de Villiers
and
Eunice van der Berg

Illustrated By
Marita Johnson

Gareth Stevens Publishing
Milwaukee

First Cookbook Library

Getting Ready To Cook
Drinks and Desserts
One Dish Meals
Vegetables and Salads
Breads and Biscuits
Cookies, Cakes, and Candies

These books will show you how easy it is to cook and what fun it is, too.

Everything you have to do is clearly illustrated and the methods you will learn are the same as those used in advanced cookbooks. Once you learn these methods, you will be able to follow recipes you find in any cookbook.

In this book you will learn how to make a tasty and nutritious meal in just one dish. Choose any one of these recipes to make a meal for your family.

If you are concerned about salt, sugar, and fats in your diet, you may reduce the amount called for or substitute other ingredients in many of the recipes. Ask a grown-up for suggestions.

More information about nutrition, ingredients, and cooking methods can be found in GETTING READY TO COOK, a companion volume to this book.

CONTENTS

Dainty Sandwiches 6

French Toast 8

Scrambled Eggs and Cheese. . . . 10

Toasted Cheese 12

Devilled Eggs. 14

Hot Dogs 16

Macaroni and Cheese 18

White Sauce. 21

Chicken à la King. 22

Tuna Casserole. 24

Baked Meatballs. 26

Tomato Beef Soup. 28

Chicken Casserole. 30

Black arrows ➡ in some recipes are reminders to ask a grown-up to help you.

Dainty Sandwiches

Take Out:

plastic bag
rolling pin
table knife

bread knife
cutting board
serving plate

What You'll Need

4 slices of bread
¼ cup soft butter
¼ cup cheese spread
½ cup flavored potato chips

1. Put the potato chips in the plastic bag. Tie it lightly and crush the chips with the rolling pin.

➡ 2. Cut off the bread crusts, so that the slices match perfectly.

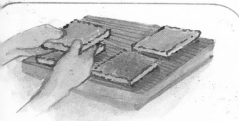

3. Spread one side of each slice with soft butter. Spread cheese spread on 2 of the 4 slices. Place the other two slices on top.

4. Spread butter over the top of each sandwich.

5. Cut each sandwich into 6 pieces with the bread knife.

6. Sprinkle the crushed potato chips on top of the butter on each sandwich.

7. Arrange the sandwiches on the serving plate and serve with tea or milk.

French Toast
(4 servings)

Take Out:

mixing bowl
egg beater
shallow dish
measuring cups
measuring spoons

spatula
frying pan
potholders
4 breakfast plates
4 knives, 4 forks

What You'll Need

3 eggs
½ cup milk
¼ teaspoon salt
4 tablespoons butter
8 slices bread
½ cup syrup or honey

1. Put the four breakfast plates in the oven to warm at 250°.

2. Break the eggs into the mixing bowl. Add the milk and salt and beat until well mixed. Pour this mixture into the shallow dish.

3. Heat the frying pan over medium heat. Melt one tablespoon of butter in the pan until it starts to bubble.

4. Dip two slices of bread, one at a time, into the egg mixture to cover both sides.

5. Use the spatula to lift the two slices into the hot frying pan. Turn them over carefully when they are light brown on one side and fry again until light brown on the other side.

6. Add another tablespoon of butter if necessary when turning the slices over. Lift the slices slightly to let the melted butter run underneath.

7. Place two slices on each breakfast plate. Keep them warm in the oven while the other slices are being fried.

8. Serve the French toast with syrup, honey, or jam.

Scrambled Eggs and Cheese
(4 servings)

Take Out:

small mixing bowl
egg beater
frying pan
wooden spoon
potholders

measuring spoons
measuring cups
4 breakfast plates
4 forks

What You'll Need

7 eggs
⅓ teaspoon salt
3 tablespoons milk

3 tablespoons butter
⅓ cup grated cheese
parsley

1. Break the eggs into the mixing bowl. Add the salt and milk and beat until well mixed.

➡ 2. Heat the frying pan over medium heat. Melt the butter in the frying pan until it bubbles.

➡3. Pour the egg mixture into the pan and turn the heat to low. Stir slowly, using the fork until the mixture thickens.
NOTE: The mixture will thicken on the bottom of the pan first. Scrape the bottom with the wooden spoon using long strokes. Take care that the egg does not boil or dry out completely.

➡ 4. Sprinkle the grated cheese over the scrambled eggs and dish it onto the four breakfast plates. Decorate each plate with a sprig of parsley.

5. Serve the eggs with toast or bread.

Toasted Cheese
(3 servings)

Take Out:

small mixing bowl
egg beater
spoon
measuring cups
measuring spoons
table knife

baking sheet
pancake turner
oven mitts
3 breakfast plates
3 knives
3 forks

What You'll Need

3 slices bread
1 cup grated cheese
1 egg
5 teaspoons melted butter
pinch of salt

1. Beat the egg with an egg beater.

2. Add the grated cheese, melted butter, and salt and mix thoroughly.

3. Divide the mixture into three equal parts.

4. Spread ⅓ evenly on each slice of bread. Place the slices on the baking sheet.

➡ 5. Put the baking sheet 4" below the oven broiler and switch on the broiler.

➡ 6. Watch the toast and remove it from the oven using the oven mitts as soon as the cheese turns golden brown. Switch off the broiler.

➡ 7. Use the pancake turner to place the toasted cheese slices on the plates and serve immediately.

Devilled Eggs
(4 servings)

Take Out:

saucepan
tablespoon
mixing bowl
small mixing bowl
measuring spoons

vegetable knife
measuring cups
fork
teaspoon
serving plate

What You'll Need

4 eggs
5 teaspoons mayonnaise
½ teaspoon prepared mustard
pinch of salt
1 teaspoon pickle relish
lettuce leaves, tomato, and parsley

1. Put the eggs in the saucepan and cover them with lukewarm water. Put on the lid and place the saucepan on the stove. Turn the heat to medium.

2. As soon as the water boils, reduce the heat to low. Simmer for 10 minutes.

3. Lift the eggs into the mixing bowl half filled with cold water. Let them cool.

4. Tap the eggs lightly to crack them and then shell them carefully. Rinse the eggs under cold running water.

5. Cut the eggs into halves lengthwise using the vegetable knife.

6. Remove the yolks and put them in the small bowl.

7. Mash the egg yolks and stir in the mayonnaise, mustard, salt, and pickle relish. If the mixture is too dry, add one teaspoon of mayonnaise at a time until the mixture is soft enough.

8. Spoon the mixture into the white halves using a teaspoon.

9. Arrange the stuffed halves on lettuce leaves with tomato wedges and sprigs of parsley.

Hot Dogs
(4 servings)

Take Out:

saucepan   tongs
bread knife   measuring spoons
table knife   4 paper plates

What You'll Need

4 hot dogs
4 hot dog buns
butter
catsup
mustard

1. Half fill the saucepan with water. Place it on the stove.

➡ 2. Turn on the burner to high and allow the water to boil.

➡ 3. Put the hot dogs into the boiling water using the tongs. Turn off the heat. Leave the hot dogs in the water for five minutes.

➡ 4. Cut the buns partly through lengthwise using the bread knife. Spread butter on both sides.

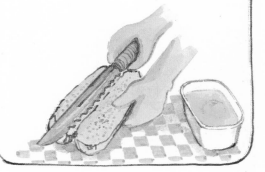

5. Spread mustard on one side and catsup on the other.

➡ 6. Put the hot dogs in the buns using the tongs.

7. Serve the hot dogs on paper plates while still hot.

Macaroni and Cheese
(4 servings)

Take Out:

2 quart casserole dish
saucepan
wooden spoon
measuring cups
measuring spoons
2 mixing bowls

slotted spoon
egg beater
colander or strainer
teaspoon
table knife
oven mitts

Recipe in two parts

Part 1

What You'll Need
½ cup macaroni
1 teaspoon salt
1 tablespoon vegetable oil

Part 2

What You'll Need
3 eggs
2 cups milk
½ teaspoon salt
¼ teaspoon dry mustard
1 cup grated American cheese
1 tablespoon butter

Part 1

➡ 1. Half fill the saucepan with hot water. Put it on the stove and turn the burner to high. Add the salt and oil when it starts to boil. Reduce the heat to medium.

➡ 2. Put the macaroni into the boiling water using the slotted spoon. Boil for 15 minutes. Stir occasionally to prevent the macaroni from sticking to the bottom of the saucepan.

➡ 3. Remove the saucepan from the stove and spoon the macaroni into the colander or strainer which is placed over a mixing bowl.

Part 2

➡ 1. Preheat the oven to 350°.

2. Grease the casserole dish.

3. Beat the eggs, salt, and mustard in the mixing bowl.

4. Add the milk and stir in the cooked macaroni and the grated cheese.

5. Pour the mixture into the casserole dish and dot with pieces of butter.

➡ 6. Bake for one hour. Use the oven mitts to remove the macaroni from the oven.

➡ 7. Insert the table knife into the dish to see if it is done. If the knife comes out clean, the mixture is done. If the mixture is milky, return the dish to the oven for another 15 minutes. Take it out and turn off the oven heat.

8. Serve with sliced tomatoes or tomato sauce.

Take Out:

measuring cups
measuring spoons
saucepan
wooden spoon
potholders

White Sauce
(1 cup)

What You'll Need

2 tablespoons butter
2 tablespoons flour
1 cup milk
½ teaspoon salt

➡ 1. Place the saucepan on the stove burner and turn the heat to low.

➡ 2. Melt the butter in the saucepan and gradually stir in the flour and salt.

➡ 3. Add the milk while stirring. Do not let the flour turn brown.

➡ 4. Continue stirring until the mixture thickens and starts to boil. Turn off the burner.

5. Use the white sauce in chicken à la king, on vegetables, or in other recipes.

Chicken à la King
(4 servings)

Take Out:

measuring spoons
measuring cups
saucepan

wooden spoon
tablespoon
oven mitts

What You'll Need

2 tablespoons butter
½ cup chopped onion
½ cup chopped celery
1 tablespoon chopped parsley
2 cups boned cooked chicken
1 cup white sauce (recipe on page 21)
4 sprigs parsley

➡ 1. Turn the burner to medium.

➡ 2. Melt the butter in the saucepan and stir in the chopped onion and celery.

➡ 3. Stir constantly until the vegetables are tender.

➡ 4. Add the chopped chicken and parsley and stir slowly until the chicken is hot.

➡ 5. Turn off the heat and leave the mixture in the saucepan while preparing the white sauce.

➡ 6. Add the chicken to the hot white sauce as soon as it is ready. Stir slowly to blend until it is hot again. Turn off the heat.

7. Serve on toast or cooked rice. Decorate each serving with a piece of parsley.

Tuna Casserole
(4 servings)

Take Out:

can opener
casserole dish (1 quart)
mixing bowl
egg beater
fork

plastic bag
rolling pin
measuring cups
oven mitts
strainer

What You'll Need

1 can cream of mushroom soup (10¾ ounces)
1 egg
⅔ cup milk
1 can tuna (6¾ ounces)
1 cup cooked or canned green peas
3 cups potato chips

→ 1. Preheat the oven to 350°.

→ 2. Open the can of soup and pour the contents into the casserole dish.

3. Beat the egg and milk together in the mixing bowl. Mix in the casserole dish using a fork.

4. Put the potato chips in a plastic bag but do not tie the bag. Crush them with the rolling pin. Add half of the crushed chips to the soup mixture.

5. Empty the tuna into the strainer held over the sink. When all the liquid is drained, flake the tuna with a fork and add it to the soup mixture.

6. Stir in the peas. Sprinkle the remaining crushed chips on top.

→ 7. Bake for 30 minutes. Use the oven mitts to remove the casserole from the oven. Turn off the oven heat.

8. Serve with a mixed green salad.

Baked Meatballs

(8 servings)

Take Out:

12 cup muffin pan
large mixing bowl
measuring cups
measuring spoons
scissors
egg beater
can opener

small mixing bowl
fork
tablespoon
vegetable knife
cutting board
serving dish
oven mitts

What You'll Need

½ cup raw oatmeal
½ cup milk
1 egg
1 package onion-mushroom soup mix (1.4 ounces)
1 pound ground round steak

➡ 1. Preheat the oven to 350°.

2. Grease the muffin cups.

3. Put the dry oatmeal in the large mixing bowl and pour the milk over.

4. Beat the egg and salt in the small mixing bowl and add it to the oatmeal and milk.

5. Cut open the soup package and shake the contents into the mixing bowl. Mix everything together with a fork.

6. Stir in the ground round steak and mix well.

7. Spoon the mixture into the muffin cups, round off the tops, and bake in the oven for ½ hour.

8. Take the pan out of the oven using the mitts. Turn off the oven heat. Arrange the meatballs in the serving dish. Serve hot with cooked rice or baked potatoes.

Tomato Beef Soup
(6 servings)

Take Out:

saucepan
measuring cups
measuring spoons
wooden spoon

strainer
mixing bowl
tablespoon
oven mitts

What You'll Need

1 tablespoon oil
½ cup chopped onion
½ cup chopped green pepper
1 pound lean ground beef
1 bay leaf
½ cup grated carrots
½ cup uncooked rice
1 tablespoon chopped parsley

½ cup milk
2 tablespoons sugar
1 tablespoon flour
1 can tomato paste (6 ounces)
½ cup water
2 teaspoons salt
1 can tomato juice (46 ounces)
¼ teaspoon oregano

➡ **NOTE:** A food processor will chop up the vegetables faster. If you have one, ask a grown-up to help you use it.

➡ 1. Measure the oil into the saucepan and heat it on the stove at a high temperature.

➡ 2. Stir-fry the chopped onion and green pepper in the oil until the onion is clear. Reduce the heat to medium.

➡ 3. Add the ground beef and stir-fry until the meat is loose and seems cooked through.

➡ 4. Add the bay leaf, carrots, rice, and milk and stir until well mixed.

5. Mix the sugar, flour, and tomato paste. Stir in the water until the mixture is smooth.

➡ 6. Add the salt and oregano. Stir it into the meat mixture in the saucepan with the wooden spoon.

➡ 7. Reduce the heat to low, put on the lid, and leave it to simmer for 30 minutes. Stir occasionally to prevent the mixture from burning. Be careful to lift the lid away from you so that the steam does not burn you.

➡ 8. Add the tomato juice, and heat for 15 more minutes.

Chicken Casserole

(4-6 servings)

Take Out:

casserole dish with cover (1½ quart)
paper towels
scissors
shallow dish

oven mitts
wooden spoon
tablespoon
cup

What You'll Need

8 chicken thighs and legs
1 package dry mushroom soup mix
1 teaspoon salt
1 cup apricot juice
1 cup fresh or canned mushrooms

➡ 1. Preheat the oven to 350°.

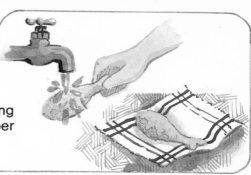

2. Wash the chicken under cold running water. Dry each piece in a paper towel.

3. Cut the package of soup open and empty it into the shallow dish.

4. Roll each thigh and leg in the dry soup mixture and arrange it in the casserole dish, placing the skin facing upwards.

5. Sprinkle the chicken with the remaining soup and salt and pour the apricot juice over it.

➡ 6. Put on the lid and place the casserole in the oven for 45 minutes.

➡ 7. Take it out of the oven. Remove the lid carefully so that the steam escapes away from you.

➡ 8. Stir in the mushrooms without breaking the chicken. Place the open casserole in the oven for another fifteen minutes.

➡ 9. Remove the casserole from the oven. Turn off the oven heat. If necessary, spoon the excess floating fat into the cup using the tablespoon.

INDEX

B
Baked meatballs 26

C
Casserole, chicken 30
Casserole, tuna 24
Cheese, macaroni and 18
Cheese, scrambled eggs and 10
Cheese, toasted 12
Chicken à la king 22
Chicken casserole 30

D
Dainty sandwiches 6
Devilled eggs 14

E
Eggs, devilled 14
Eggs, scrambled 10

F
French toast 8

H
Hot dogs 16

M
Macaroni and cheese 18
Meatballs, baked 26

S
Sauce, white 21
Scrambled eggs and cheese 10
Soup, tomato beef 28

T
Toasted cheese 12
Toast, French 8
Tomato beef soup 28
Tuna casserole 24

W
White sauce 21

Black arrows ➡ in some recipes are reminders to ask a grown-up to help you.